MEMPHIS
The Delaplaine 2017 Long Weekend Guide

No business listed in this guide has provided *anything* free to be included.

Andrew Delaplaine

A list of the author's other travel guides, as well as his political thrillers and titles for children, can be found at the end of this book.

Senior Editors
Renee & Sophie Delaplaine

Senior Writer
James Cubby

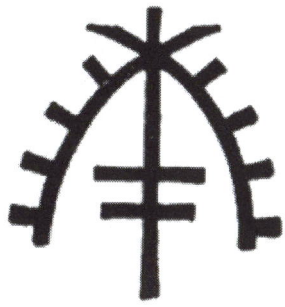

Gramercy Park Press
New York – London - Paris

Copyright © by Gramercy Park Press - All rights reserved.

Please submit corrections, additions or comments to
andrewdelaplaine@mac.com

MEMPHIS
The Delaplaine 2017 Long Weekend Guide

TABLE OF CONTENTS

Chapter 1 – WHY MEMPHIS? – 4

Chapter 2 – WHERE TO STAY – 7
High on the Hog – Sensible Alternatives – Budget

Chapter 3 – WHERE TO EAT – 15
Extravagant – Middle Ground – Budget

Chapter 4 – NIGHTLIFE – 41

Chapter 5 – WHAT TO SEE & DO – 49

Chapter 6 – SHOPPING & SERVICES- 62

INDEX – 70

OTHER BOOKS BY THE SAME AUTHOR – 73

Chapter 1
WHY MEMPHIS?

Though Memphis is the biggest city in Tennessee, Nashville is the capital. There's always been something of a rivalry between the two cities.

Nashville may be claim to be "Music Capital of the World," but Memphis is almost universally recognized as the home of the Blues.

And Elvis? Where did the King choose to live? Memphis has **Graceland**, Elvis Presley's big mansion that draws tens of thousands of visitors a year.

Like many another city I've covered, Memphis has rediscovered its Downtown area after leaving it to rot for decades. New businesses are thriving, artists are creating exciting storefronts and galleries, the retail scene is getting more interesting, new bars are popping up.

Memphis also is developing as a center for innovative cuisine, not as advanced as Nashville is (yet), but things are happening.

One thing you can do in Memphis just about cheaper than you can anywhere else is eat some of the best BBQ to be found in America. There are countless places serving up Memphis style BBQ. (Actually, I did count once, and there are about 75 BBQ places in the area.) There are dozens of places where it's hard to spend more than $10 for a meal consisting of a pulled pork sandwich, a side of fries and a soft drink or iced tea. I haven't seen this miracle anywhere else. I mean, I can show you how to eat cheap even in New York, but unless you're in Queens, where there are hundreds of fine ethnic eateries, you have to seek out the best places.

As I wrote after visiting **Payne's Original Bar-B-Que** in the listings below, when you say BBQ in Memphis, you mean pork shoulder, not ribs so much. Every little joint has its own "secret" method of handling the fire and wood.

The pork is always slow-roasted and then "pulled" by hand from the bone or chopped with the kind of cleavers you see in horror movies. The resultant pile of savory meat is placed on any of dozens of types of hamburger style buns and then topped with a dollop of coleslaw. Sauce is either added or it's not, depending on the place you're visiting. I have often spent my entire trip in Memphis eating nothing but BBQ.

And not regretted it one minute.

My last word of advice: you won't either.

Chapter 2
WHERE TO STAY

PRICELINE and **HOTWIRE**
www.priceline.com
www.hotwire.com
With Priceline, you bid on rooms in the part of the city where you want to stay, select whatever star levels you want, and generally can get cheaper rooms. These are usually in hotel chains, so nothing with too much character. With Hotwire, they tell you the price of the room. You don't bid on it. You can often play one site off against the other to get an even cheaper deal. (You don't find out the name of the lodging until you close the deal.)

JAMES LEE HOUSE
690 Adams Ave, Memphis, 901-359-6750
www.jamesleehouse.com
NEIGHBORHOOD: Victorian Village
This historic bed and breakfast (built in 1848 and once an arts conservatory) offers guests luxurious and comfortable accommodations. This opulent home features five beautifully appointed suites. You won't believe when you walk into this place that it was only restored in 2014, and many Victorian highlights were brought back to life: the frescoed ceiling, elaborate golden Victorian cornices and mirrors, the intricate moldings, distressed fireplaces. But thoroughly modern touches are welcome, like the TempurPedic mattresses and rain showers. Amenities include: free gourmet breakfast with made-to-order eggs, gated private parking, large LED cable TVs, and free wireless Internet access.

THE MADISON HOTEL
79 Madison Ave, Memphis, 901-333-1200
www.madisonhotelmemphis.com
NEIGHBORHOOD: Downtown
Located in a downtown high-rise, this four-diamond hotel offers 110 guest rooms, many with river views. The fairly new hotel luxury boutique hotel boasts a cool urban design with modern furnishings and upscale lodgings. Working through the Memphis Artists Spotlight program, they display the work of local artists in the public rooms. This building used to be a bank. The gym in the basement is in the 100-year-old vault. Amenities include: 24-hour room service, wireless high-speed internet access, valet laundry, private wine reserves, spa inspired rain showers, 37" flat screen LCD TVs, and Keurig coffee makers. On-site dining available at **Eighty3**, an upscale eatery with a globally inspired menu. The hotel's **Twilight Sky Terrace** rooftop serves handcrafted cocktails and light bites, not to mention superior views of the Mighty Mississippi. On-site 30-foot lap pool.

PEABODY HOTEL
149 Union Ave, Memphis, 901-529-4000
www.peabodymemphis.com
This luxury hotel is known for the "Peabody Ducks" that make daily treks to the lobby from the rooftop. Here guests experience the historic opulence and Southern hospitality befitting a four-Diamond hotel in its 464 smoke-free deluxe guest rooms, including 15 luxurious suites. Amenities include: Pet-friendly rooms available, heated indoor pool and day spa, athletic club, in-room dining, complete audiovisual services, free newspaper, 42" flat screen TV with premium cable stations and on-command movies, and high-speed wireless internet access. On-site dining available at Peabody's award-winning restaurants, bars, and eateries. The Peabody offers a variety of boutiques including The Lucky Duck that specializes in duck-themed items.

ROULHAC MANSION
810 E McLemore Ave, Memphis, 901-775-1665
NEIGHBORHOOD:
As the premier Bed & Breakfast in Memphis, this mansion offers six luxurious guest room on two-levels. Amenities include: free internet access, free parking, cable/satellite TV, free local calls, in-room mini bars, night club, non-smoking rooms, and wake-up service. No swimming pool and no pets allowed. Free southern breakfast.

THE SLEEP INN AT COURT SQUARE
40 N Front St, Memphis, 901-522-9700
www.choicehotels.com/tennessee/memphis/sleep-inn-hotels
NEIGHBORHOOD: Downtown
The hotel offers 124 comfortable (and quite affordable) rooms in an ideal location. You have the river on one side and the Main Street pedestrian mall and Court Square Park on the other side. Amenities

include: cable/satellite TVs, flat screen/plasma TVs, coffee makers, free wireless high-speed Internet access, free morning breakfast, and free daily newspaper weekdays. Conveniently located near attractions like Mud Island River Park, Beale Street, and Graceland. A Smoke-free hotel.

THE TALBOT HEIRS
99 South Second St, 800-955-3956 or 901-527-9772
www.talbotheirs.com
NEIGHBORHOOD: Downtown
Located in the heart of downtown Memphis, this unique guesthouse features 7 spacious suites, each totally different, with kitchens. (You'll have to use the stairs.) Amenities include: CD player, cable TV with HBO and other movie channels, coffee maker, and free high-speed internet access. Snacks, juice, milk, coffee, and tea are provided each day. Exercise equipment (stationary bike, stepper, and treadmill) available for use within your suite. Conveniently located near local attractions, museums, restaurants, and nightlife.

Chapter 3
WHERE TO EAT

A & R BAR-B-QUE
NEIGHBORHOOD: East Memphis
3721 Hickory Hill Rd, Memphis, 901-365-9777
NEIGHBORHOOD: Whitehaven
1802 Elvis Presley Blvd, Memphis, 901-774-7444
www.aandrbbq.com
CUISINE: Barbeque
DRINKS: No Booze
SERVING: Lunch & Dinner daily
PRICE RANGE: $
Even though I rhapsodize about the "pulled" or "chopped" pork shoulder sandwiches that make Memphis BBQ so unique in other restaurants, here I always go for the Memphis style ribs. They are just

out of this world. Hold up a rib and give it a little shake and the meat will fall off. It's that tender and juicy. Be sure you order the dry version (no sauce) so you can fully absorb the complex flavors that went into this dish. (You can add sauce later.)

ALCENIA'S
317 N Main St, 901-523-0200
www.alcenias.com
CUISINE: Soul Food, Desserts
DRINKS: No Booze
SERVING: 9 – 5 Tuesday-Saturday; closed Sunday & Monday; late breakfast or lunch
PRICE RANGE: $
NEIGHBORHOOD: Uptown
Owner Alcenia's daughter often welcomes guests with a hug, making it a popular place among locals. The menu features home-style soul food. Menu favorites include: Salmon croquettes, Chicken and waffles, and if you want fried chicken, skip it and get the baked chicken; the bread pudding, the custard pie and the sweet potato pie are the standouts on the

dessert menu. Also, when was the last time you walked into a restaurant where the owner hugged you?

ARCADE RESTAURANT
540 South Main St, 901-526-5757
www.arcaderestaurant.com
CUISINE: Southern Diner
DRINKS: No Booze
SERVING: Breakfast & Lunch (7 to 3 daily)
PRICE RANGE: $
NEIGHBORHOOD: Downtown
Located in the center of the historic district, this restaurant (it's really a diner, not so much a "restaurant") takes you back in time. It's got booths upholstered in squeaky plastic against the windows and those uncomfortable bar stools at the counter that are riveted to the floor so you can't move them. But as painful as they are on my big butt, I always sit at the counter when I can so you can talk to the

waitresses, which is half the fun. Several films were shot here: "Great Balls of Fire," "The Client," "The Firm," "Walk the Line" and "21 Grams," among them. Avoid the weekends for breakfast if you can, as it gets pretty crowded. The Southern breakfasts are a big hit here (think sweet potato pancakes with eggs and grits). Menu favorites include: Chicken and Dumplings and Chicken Spaghetti. A wide range of sandwiches, salads and pizzas for lunch. Or get what was said to be Elvis's favorite sandwich: fried peanut butter & banana. (Makes me want to puke.)

ALCHEMY BAR
940 South Cooper St, Memphis, 901-726-4444
www.alchemymemphis.com
CUISINE: Tapas
DRINKS: Full Bar
SERVING: Dinner nightly and Lunch only on Sunday
PRICE RANGE: $$$
NEIGHBORHOOD: Cooper-Young
A casual hipster eatery featuring a simple menu of Tapas and New American cuisine. Menu favorites include: Chili Roasted Fish Tacos and Coriander Crusted Lamb Chop. Great choice for brunch. Gluten-free options available.

ANDREW MICHAEL ITALIAN KITCHEN
712 W Brookhaven Cir, Memphis, 901-347-3569
www.andrewmichaelitaliankitchen.com
CUISINE: Italian
DRINKS: Full Bar
SERVING: Dinner; closed Sun & Mon

PRICE RANGE: $$$
This Beard Award Semi-Finalist is touted as Memphis' most celebrated restaurant. Menu features many Italian favorites and specialties like Duck with root vegetables. Great dessert choices like the Maple Tart. Menu changes daily.

THE BAR-B-Q SHOP
1782 Madison Ave, Memphis, 901-272-1277
www.dancingpigs.com
CUISINE: Barbeque
DRINKS: Beer & Wine Only
SERVING: Lunch & Dinner
PRICE RANGE: $$
NEIGHBORHOOD: Midtown
This place is home to the famous **Dancing Pigs BBQ** sauce and seasoning and it's known as "Best in Memphis." If you're into spicy BBQ, then this is your place. (It's done in a Buffalo style.) The menu offers

items like spicy ribs and pulled pork sandwich. (They use Texas toast instead of a bun, which is nice.) If you like the sauce, they sell it to go.

BAR DKDC
964 South Cooper St, Memphis, 901-272-0830
www.bardkdc.com
CUISINE: Tapas
DRINKS: Full Bar
SERVING: Dinner; closed Sun & Mon
PRICE RANGE: $$
NEIGHBORHOOD: Cooper-Young
This bar offers Chef Karen Carrier's eclectic menu of local cuisines and international street food. Nice cocktails. Menu changes often. Live music on the weekends.

THE BEAUTY SHOP RESTAURANT
966 Cooper St, Memphis, 901-272-7111
www.thebeautyshoprestaurant.com
CUISINE: Caribbean/American
DRINKS: Full Bar
SERVING: Lunch & Dinner
PRICE RANGE: $$
NEIGHBORHOOD: Cooper-Young
Located in a former '60s beauty parlor, this kitschy New American eatery offers a menu as fun as the décor. Dinner favorites include: Grilled Espresso Honey Lamb Loin Chops and Sugar & Spiced Peking Duck. Great choice for Sunday Brunch.

BRAD'S BAR-B-Q
2845 Bartlett Rd, Bartlett, Tenn., 901-373-6326
No Website
CUISINE: Barbeque
DRINKS: No Booze
SERVING: Lunch & Dinner
PRICE RANGE: $$
NEIGHBORHOOD: Bartlett
Just across the Tennessee border (but only about 20 minutes from Downtown Memphis) you'll find the infamous Memphis-style dry rub BBQ that keeps people coming back for more. Everything seems to come with sides like juicy baked beans, spicy may saw, potato spears and greasy onion rings. No booze here but delicious sweet iced tea.

BROTHER JUNIPER'S
9514 Walker Ave, Memphis, 901-324-0144
www.brotherjunipers.com
CUISINE: BreakfastAmerican
DRINKS: No Booze
SERVING: Breakfast & Lunch
PRICE RANGE: $$
This is a total old school diner that serves only breakfast and lunch. Typical diner fare. Their fried chicken recipe is carefully guarded.

CORKY'S RIBS & BBQ
5259 Poplar Ave, Memphis, 901-685-9744
www.corkysmemphis.com
CUISINE: Barbeque
DRINKS: Full Bar
SERVING: Lunch & Dinner

PRICE RANGE: $$
NEIGHBORHOOD: Eastgate
Here the BBQ meats are slow cooked over hickory wood and charcoal. This place is more "commercial" than a lot of the other joints in town. Slicker. Try the hand pulled pork sandwich served hot with cole slaw – it might be the best deal in Memphis.

CENTRAL BBQ
NEIGHBORHOOD: Midtown
2249 Central Ave, Memphis, 901-272-9377
NEIGHBORHOOD: Downtown
147 E Butler, Memphis, 901-672-7760
NEIGHBORHOOD: East
4375 Summer, Memphis, 901-767-4672
www.cbqmemphis.com
CUISINE: Barbeque
DRINKS: Beer & Wine Only
SERVING: Lunch & Dinner
PRICE RANGE: $$

Central has taken top honors in the ever-ongoing "Best BBQ in Memphis" sweepstakes about a dozen times. What do they do? They "slow smoke" all their meats: ribs, pork, chicken, turkey, beef brisket, sausage and bologna. Their premium meats are rubbed with a secret combination of dry spices, marinated for 24 hours, then smoked low and slow in the pit over a combination of hickory and pecan woods. No sauce is ever introduced into the pit. (Whatever you order, start with their smoked hot chicken wings.) The meat here is piled higher than in most other BBQ joints. If you opt for the pork plate, see if they can give you "extra bark." That's the extra thick crust on the meat that brings with it a heavy smokiness you'll love. You'll also like the young, lively crowd that comes here from the nearby colleges. Take home an order of their homemade potato chips. They are specially cut thick and they are "salted" with a house blend that's completely unique and mouthwatering.

CHARLIE VERGOS' RENDEZVOUS
52 S 2nd St, Memphis, 901-523-2746
www.hogsfly.com
CUISINE: Barbeque
DRINKS: Beer & Wine Only
SERVING: 4:30 to 10:30 Tuesday-Thursday; 11 to 11 Friday & Saturday; closed Sunday & Monday
PRICE RANGE: $$
NEIGHBORHOOD: Downtown

Here the ribs are not wet and they're not dry. Charlie Vergos opened this place in 1948. He was Greek, and as part of his special recipe, just before they serve the ribs, they baste them in a vinegar-based marinade and then sprinkle a blend of spices over the meat. Charlie died in 2010, but he left the place to his kids who make the ribs the same way Charlie did. There's nothing quite like in anywhere in town. This place is in a basement down an alleyway in Downtown, but once you go in, you'll see how big it is. And the "rendezvous" is not just a tagline. Everybody comes here eventually, whether you're the president or a Rolling Stone. Lots of interesting memorabilia on the walls, too. (They've developed a huge mail-order business and deliver their BBQ to you by Fedex.)

COZY CORNER
735 N Parkway, Memphis, 901-527-9158
www.cozycornerbbq.com
CUISINE: Barbeque
DRINKS: Beer & Wine Only

SERVING: 11 to 9 Tuesday-Saturday
PRICE RANGE: $$
NEIGHBORHOOD: Midtown
The BBQ is authentic at this little storefront shop with a self-service counter and a small dining room. What's really special here (and you won't find this anywhere else in Memphis but here) is the whole Cornish hen that is BBQ-ed to perfection. So moist and flavorful. The rib tips are the other thing I like here after the Cornish hen. The spare ribs are roasted over charcoal until tender but some folks say the best dish in the house is the barbecued baloney. (Not me. I think it's disgusting.)

THE FOUR WAY
998 Mississippi Blvd, 901-507-1519
www.fourwaymemphis.com
CUISINE: Soul Food, Southern

DRINKS: No Booze
SERVING: Lunch & Dinner (11 till 7 p.m., but only 5 p.m. Saturday); closed Monday
PRICE RANGE: $
NEIGHBORHOOD: Southside
This historic soul food restaurant (since 1946) serves great Southern dishes like fried catfish and turkey and dressing. Menu favorites include: Salmon Croquet; Liver & Onions; and Country Fried Steak. The sides are great: smothered cabbage (I could make a meal of this alone); turnip greens; fried green tomatoes; boiled okra; broccoli & cheese. Peach cobbler for dessert unless you go for the lemon meringue pie.

GIBSON DONUTS
760 Mt Moriah Rd, Memphis, 901-682-8200
CUISINE: Donuts & Bagels
DRINKS: No Booze
SERVING: 24 Hours
PRICE RANGE: $
NEIGHBORHOOD: Midtown
This donut shop, making donuts since 1967, offers a larger variety than most. There's plenty of seating so you can grab a donut or bagel with some coffee and chill. The varieties of donuts here is amazing including: chocolate filled, apple pie, red velvet, and maple bacon.

GUS'S WORLD FAMOUS FRIED CHICKEN
310 S Front St Memphis, 901-527-4877
www.gusfriedchicken.com
CUISINE: Southern
DRINKS: Beer & Wine Only

SERVING: Lunch & Dinner
PRICE RANGE: $
NEIGHBORHOOD: Downtown
This place has been serving fried chicken for almost 60 years, not at this location, but the locals love it and keep the place packed. There is a wait and it's one of those old-school blues-infused Southern spots. The menu offers fried chicken and a variety of sides, and nothing else. Nothing. No frills here.

HOG & HOMINY
707 W Brookhaven Cir, Memphis, 901-207-7396
www.hogandhominy.com
CUISINE: Italian, Southern
DRINKS: Full Bar
SERVING: Lunch & Dinner daily
PRICE RANGE: $$
NEIGHBORHOOD: Brennan

This relaxed eatery situated in a renovated private home has a bocce court on one side and a steel beer tub bar out back that makes you feel like you might have stumbled into a frat party. But the food is dead serious, offering a unique mix of Italian and Southern cuisine. Where else can you get pork rinds made to order along with gnocchi? Somehow, it works. The simple menu features lots of product from local farmers. Buffalo-style pork tails; meatballs with guanciale, Parmesan; several pizzas—I liked the Red Eye best: pork belly, egg, Fontina, celery leaf. If you can handle it, the only dessert you should even think about is their peanut butter pie. Sickeningly good. The bar focuses on bourbons and creative cocktails. No reservations. This is the irreverent neighbor to **Andrew Michael Italian Kitchen** across the street at No. 712 that the owners of the H&H opened first, in 2008.

IRIS
2146 Monroe Ave, Memphis, 901-590-2828

www.restaurantiris.com
CUISINE: French; Cajun; Creole
DRINKS: Full bar
SERVING: Dinner nightly except Sunday, when its closed
PRICE RANGE: $$$
NEIGHBORHOOD: Midtown
The celebrated chef here is a guy named Kelly English, and his menu reflects his upbringing in southern Louisiana. He's become one of the most respected chefs in Memphis and won lots of awards. Iris is situated in a lovingly restored mid-century home. This place is located near historic Overton Square. Though the menu changes based on what's available locally different times of the year, expect items like: All spice seared duck breast; lobster "knuckle sandwich"; slow roasted lamb belly with charred corn; veal schnitzel with truffled mashed potatoes. Chef's menu also available, which is what I suggest you opt for. The chef has another restaurant right next door, a little less formal, called the **Second Line,** which is just as good in an entirely different way. Second Line is also a lot easier to get into than Iris. They share the same kitchen.

LAS TORTUGAS DELI MEXICANA
1215 S Germantown Rd, Germantown, 901-751-1200
www.delimexicana.com
CUISINE: Mexican
DRINKS: Beer & Wine Only
SERVING: Lunch & Dinner; closed Sun
PRICE RANGE: $$
NEIGHBORHOOD: Germantown

Casual café specializing in Mexican street food. Menu favorites include: De Carnitas Mexico City made with barbecue pork and their Tacos. Bread baked fresh daily, which makes their Mexicans sandwiches so delectable. Fresh fruit juices are splendid and served with shaved ice. Worth the trip alone is the homemade guacamole, which explains why a lot of area chefs trek out here on their day off to eat such authentic food.

LAFAYETTE'S MUSIC ROOM
2119 Madison Ave, Memphis, 901-207-5097
www.lafayettes.com/memphis
CUISINE: American
DRINKS: Full Bar
SERVING: Lunch & Dinner
PRICE RANGE: $$
NEIGHBORHOOD: Midtown
Local restaurant/bar that serves Southern food with an attitude. Indoor—outdoor club features bands 7 nights a week. This is the place that helped launch the careers of such luminaries as Billy Joel, Big Star and KISS. Closed for many years, it reopened in 2014.

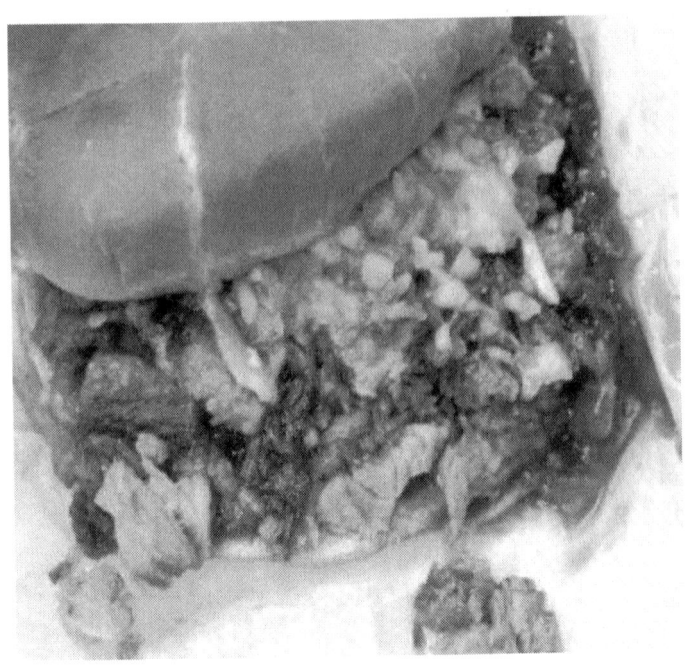

PAYNE'S ORIGINAL BAR-B-QUE
1762 Lamar Ave, Memphis, 901-272-1523
No web site
CUISINE: Barbeque
DRINKS: No Booze
SERVING: Lunch & Dinner
PRICE RANGE: $ - **cash only**
NEIGHBORHOOD: Med District

On your way into town from the airport is this place that's been serving BBQ for decades in what used to be an old gas station. No frills, but damned fine food. Even the side dishes are missing here. It's all about the BBQ. You have to bear in mind that in Memphis BBQ doesn't mean ribs—it means pork shoulder. Specifically, pork shoulder that's been pulled off the bone and often chopped up and served with cole slaw on a bun. Sauce is either mild or hot. "One chopped hot" is what you want to order at Payne's. It's something in the slaw that goes with this pork sandwich that makes it so delicious. And if the chop is just right, you'll get a little crunchy crust mixed in with the moist meat. There's a unique sweetness to the sauce here that is unlike any other I've tasted in Memphis. Call up to make a to-go order and you'll hear the fine sound of chop-chop-chopping in the background. Cash only.

THE SECOND LINE
2144 Monroe Ave, Memphis, 901-590-2829
www.secondlinememphis.com
CUISINE: Cajun/Creole, Comfort Food
DRINKS: Full Bar
SERVING: Dinner nightly; lunch on weekends
PRICE RANGE: $$
NEIGHBORHOOD: Midtown
Located in a redesigned house from mid-century, this place is always busy and there's usually a wait. It's not as fancy as its next door neighbor owned by the same chef, Chef Kelly English, Iris, which is much more formal than this place. Here the emphasis is on down home comfort food from southern Louisiana: Po'boys (several types: fried shrimp; braised chicken thighs & Swiss, which is my personal favorite; beef & gravy; catfish, BBQ shrimp); Andouille, crawfish & Pimento cheese Fries; seafood platters; fried oyster salad; crabmeat and corn hushpuppies. The heart-and-soul of Second Line is the bar, where the cocktails are handcrafted, each one made to order, including the

fresh-squeezed juices. (There's a nice patio out back as well.) The food is just a fantastic add-on to what would be a great bar if it didn't have food.

SOUL FISH CAFÉ
4720 Poplar Ave, Memphis, 901-590-0323
www.soulfishcafe.com
CUISINE: Seafood
DRINKS: Beer & Wine Only
SERVING: Lunch & Dinner
PRICE RANGE: $$
NEIGHBORHOOD: Brennan
This seafood eatery offers great Southern dishes like Fried Catfish and Po'boys made with Gambino bread from New Orleans. Menu favorites include: Soul Fish Platter and Smoked Pork chops. Popular family dining destination with children's menu.

SWEET GRASS
937 Cooper St, Memphis, 901-278-0278
www.sweetgrassmemphis.com
CUISINE: Southern with some Italian
DRINKS: Full Bar
SERVING: Dinner nightly except Monday, when it's closed; also brunch on Sunday
PRICE RANGE: $$
NEIGHBORHOOD: Cooper-Young
This small neighborhood bistro serves Low Country style cuisine with local ingredients, made by a chef who was a recent "Food & Wine" magazine best chef nominee. Chef Ryan Trimm's grandmother was Italian, and she taught him right. The place is a comfortable size with a bar that seats 8-10. The work of local artists is displayed on a rotating basis. If the weather's good, try for a seat on the patio outside. Menu favorites include: Braised Pork Cheeks; Mustard Glazed Grouper; osso bucco; housemade

charcuterie platters with items like pork tongue paté, kielbasa, Cajun ham, liver loaf.

THREE LITTLE PIGS
5145 Quince Rd, Memphis, 901-685-7094
www.threelittlepigsbar-b-q.com
CUISINE: Barbeque
DRINKS: No
SERVING: Lunch & Dinner
PRICE RANGE:
NEIGHBORHOOD: Eastgate
A few minutes out of town is this cute little roadside BBQ spot is a locals' favorite serving Memphis-style pork shoulder barbeque. Great place for a quick lunch or to order food for the family to go. This is also a great stop for breakfast. Their motto is memorable: "We will Serve No Swine Before Its Time."

TOM'S BAR-B-Q & DELI
4087 New Getwell Rd, Memphis, 901-365-6690

www.tomsbarbeque.com
CUISINE: Barbeque
DRINKS: No Booze
SERVING: Lunch & Dinner, Closed Sunday
PRICE RANGE: $
NEIGHBORHOOD: Oakhaven
In business for over 30 years and is home to the World Famous Rib Tips. (Rib tips are created when ribs are cut St. Louis style. They're just leftovers. But they are delicious, almost like chewy pieces of crunchy leather, but oh, so good.) Menu includes items like: Jumbo hot wings, BBQ chicken, pork chops, and beef brisket. It's a dive but the food is spectacular. Try the Channel Catfish Sandwich - it's a winner

TOPS BAR-B-Q
6130 Macon Rd, Memphis, 901-371-0580
4183 Summer Ave, Memphis, 901-324-4325
2288 Frayser Blvd, Memphis, 901-353-4925
1383 Jackson Ave, Memphis, 901-274-8600
www.topsbarbq.com
CUISINE: Barbeque
DRINKS: No Booze
SERVING: Lunch & Dinner
PRICE RANGE: $
NEIGHBORHOOD: Barlett
Here's your simple fast food BBQ joint for those needing a quick BBQ fix. This place celebrated their 60th anniversary in 2012 so they're doing something right. Menu features variety of Bar-B-Q items like ribs, brisket, and also offers great hamburgers. Wherever you are in Memphis, you're likely close to

one of these places. (I've only listed 4 locations above—there are a few more.) Their hickory-flavored chopped BBQ sandwich topped with a coleslaw that's pungent with mustard is what you want to order.

TSUNAMI
928 Cooper St, Memphis, 901-274-2556
www.tsunamimemphis.com
CUISINE: Seafood/Tapas
DRINKS: Full Bar
SERVING: Dinner; closed Sun
PRICE RANGE: $$
NEIGHBORHOOD: Midtown
Popular eatery that offers a great menu of Pacific Rim small plates. Menu changes with the seasons.

YOUNG AVENUE DELI
2119 Young Ave, Memphis, 901-278-0034
www.youngavenuedeli.com
CUISINE: Deli
DRINKS: Full Bar
SERVING: Lunch & Dinner
PRICE RANGE: $
NEIGHBORHOOD: Cooper-Young
Basically a bar featuring live music but they do offer a menu of lots of delicious salads and sandwiches.

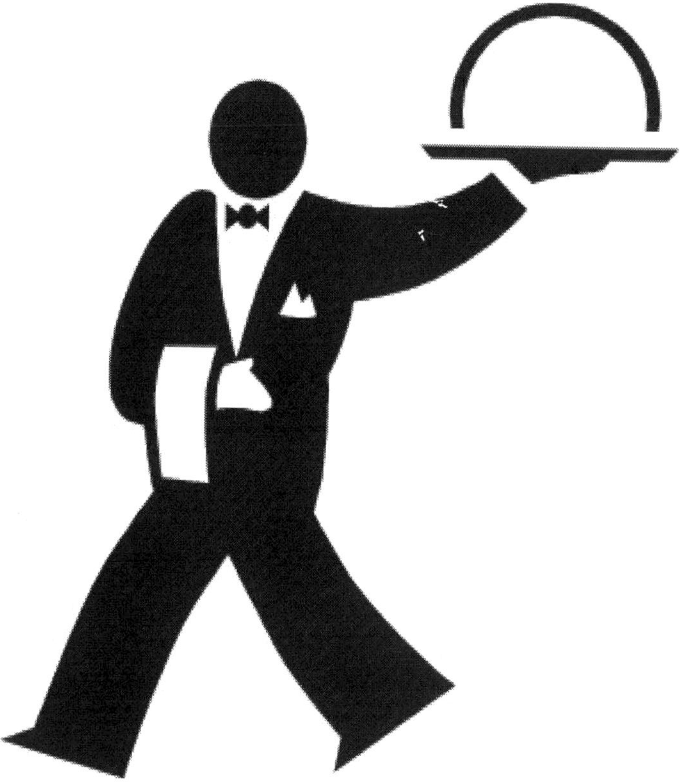

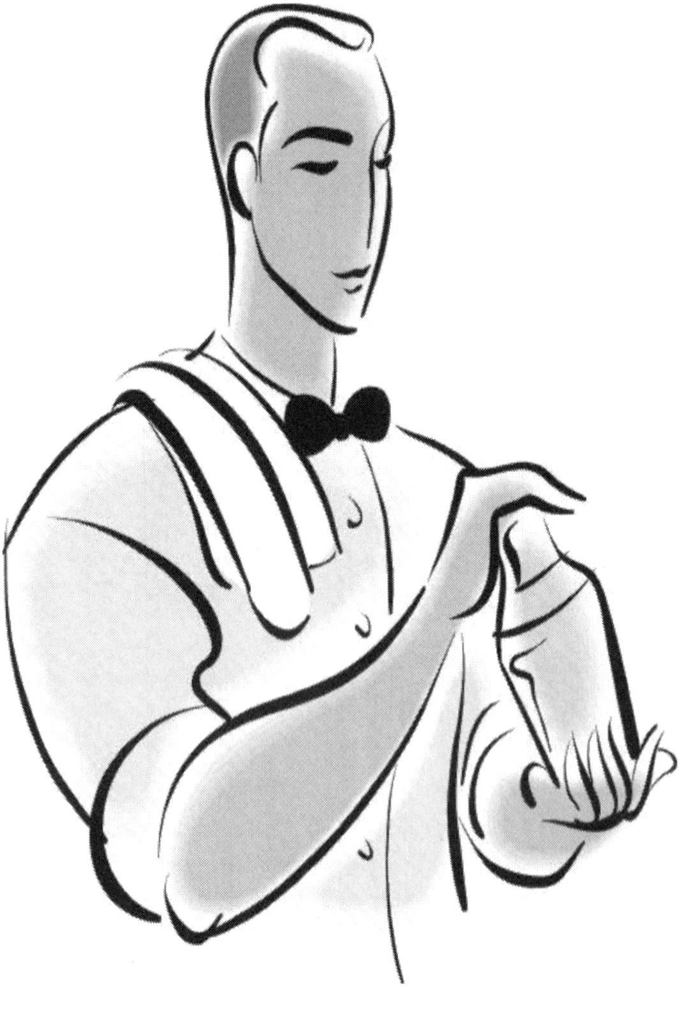

Chapter 4
NIGHTLIFE

You've probably heard that Beale Street is the "Home of the Blues." And it is. You'll find an endless line of bars and lounges, a dizzying array of live music being offered in a lot of them. Pedestrians flock to the street at night and take it over, probably because they're allowed to drink as they stroll alone, picking up new drinks from each new place they pass. It's downright sinful.

Beale Street runs on for a bit, but the busiest portion is really quite small. You'll be surprised.

It had been the center of black life long ago, but hit a downturn that resulted in the whole street being abandoned, businesses boarded up and left to rot. It was reclaimed beginning in the 1980s when the city purchased a lot of the buildings and the revival began in spurts.

Now, millions of visitors come here to revel in the nightlife and music.

Beware Saturday night from 11 p.m. to 5 a.m. Sunday—this is the most dangerous time to be on Beale Street. The city still hasn't been able to curtail the violence.

CLUB 152 ON BEALE
152 Beale St, Memphis, 901-544-7011
www.club152memphis.com
NEIGHBORHOOD: Downtown
This big club on Beale Street offers 3 floors of entertainment—you've got pretty much everything you're looking for: live entertainment in the form of touring bands, local blues bands, local DJs serving up a wide range of dance music. The first floor has live entertainment 7 nights a week. On the second floor, DJs work the crowd into a frenzy with hip hop and other types of music (Friday and Saturday). On the third floor, which opens at midnight on Friday and Saturday, another DJ performs.

CLUB RUMBA
303 S Main St, Memphis, 901-523-0020
www.memphisrumbaroom.com / web site down at press time
NEIGHBORHOOD: Downtown
A great place to slip into to dance with professional dancers if you don't have someone with you. Live band, salsa dancing, a bar. Small cover.

HAMMER & ALE
921 S Cooper, Memphis, 901-410-8223
www.hammerandale.com
NEIGHBORHOOD: Cooper-Young / Note: no cash; debit or credit cards only and they won't even run a tab. Go figure.
One of the best places in town known for its wide selection of craft beers on tap, including locally made brews.

KINGS PALACE CAFE'S ABSINTHE ROOM

162 Beale St, Memphis, 901-521-1851
www.kingspalacecafe.com
An intimate bar that specializes in absinthe. Follow the psychedelic staircase up to this unique bar that features 3 pool rooms, 2 overlooking Beale Street.

MOLLIE FONTAINE LOUNGE
679 Adams Ave, Memphis, 901-524-1886
www.molliefontainelounge.com
NEIGHBORHOOD: Downtown
Has a little bit of everything going on here, from the serene piano bar downstairs where someone will be playing and singing to an upstairs room which is more lounge-like to a clubby scene with a DJ to a restaurant serving very nice food. All located in an old Victorian manse once inhabited by the eponymous Mollie Fontaine.

RUM BOOGIE CAFÉ
182 Beale St, Memphis, 91-528-0150
http://rumboogie.com

NEIGHBORHOOD: Downtown
Their motto here is, "Eat, Drink, Boogie, Repeat." And that pretty much sums it up. Come for the music, the great selection of rums and beer, since you're down here on Beale Street, but skip the BBQ. There are too many other great BBQ places in Memphis to eat it here.

PAULA AND RAIFORD'S DISCO
14 S 2nd St, Memphis, 901-521-2494
http://paularaifords.com/home.html
NEIGHBORHOOD: Downtown
Great dancing in this 2-level club with great music, relaxing couches, a fog machine, busy DJs.

SILLY GOOSE
100 Peabody Pl, Memphis, 901-435-6915
www.sillygoosememphis.com
NEIGHBORHOOD: Downtown

A good option for dancing to DJs and craft cocktails in this hip and trendy lounge. Has a modest menu of snacks and a couple of sandwiches (burgers, pulled pork), pizzas.

WILD BILL'S
1580 Vollintine Ave, Memphis, 901-207-3975
No Website
NEIGHBORHOOD: Vollintine
This club is legendary for the live blues acts and has hosted everyone from B.B. King to Buddy Guy. One good way to save on wall treatments and décor? Let everybody and his cousin tack up their own pictures, like prisoners who want to leave a memorial that they

were here. They only serve beer, big beers, the 40-ounce size. They also have a great house band, an open kitchen, a friendly bar, and a small dance floor. Modest cover charge. Cash only.

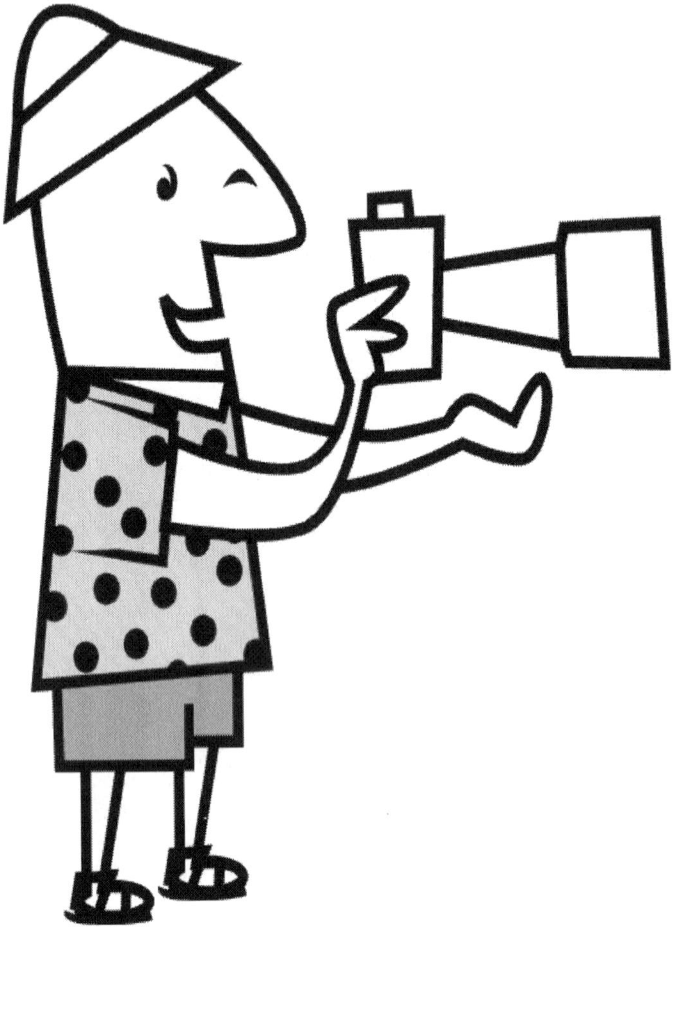

Chapter 5
WHAT TO SEE & DO

AUTOZONE PARK
200 Union Ave, Downtown Memphis, 901-721-6000
www.milb.com/index.jsp?sid=t235
The Cardinals Triple-A affiliate plays in this lovely park located in the heart of Downtown Memphis, AutoZone Park was named the 2009 Minor League Ballpark of the Year by *Baseball America*. By combining the feel of such parks as Wrigley Field, Fenway Park, and Camden Yards, AutoZone Park is a state-of-the-art facility with classic, neo-traditional style.

BACKBEAT TOURS
BB KING'S BLUE'S CLUB
143 Beale St, Memphis, 901-527-2415

www.backbeattours.com
This company offers a variety of tour from the highly rated Memphis Mojo Tour (a combination of live music, comedy, an narration that takes you through Memphis' musical heritage) to the popular Graceland Tour. Other tours available: Memphis Discovery Tour, Historic Memphis Walking Tour, and the Memphis Ghost Tour. Tours are a step-on service but private tours are available. Rates vary depending on tour.

FULL GOSPEL TABERNACLE CHURCH
787 Hale Road, Memphis, 901-396-9192
No Website
NEIGHBORHOOD: Whitehaven
Started by Al Green in 1979, this is a popular church for visitors who often take up half the pews. Here you'll hear some exciting gospel but the main attraction is the Reverend Al Green. Services are at 11:15. Dress properly if you go.

GRACELAND
3734 Elvis Presley Blvd, Memphis, 901-332-3322
www.graceland.com
NEIGHBORHOOD: Whitehaven
Home of Elvis Presley, "The King of Rock and Roll." It's no surprise that this is the No. 1 tourist attraction in Memphis. (It's the second most visited private residence in the USA, topped only by something called the White House.)

Think "tacky tourist" trap but don't miss it—you might be pleasantly surprised. Although it is not advisable to venture in the suburbs surrounding the site, there are lots and lots of Elvis-related stuff to see here—the house itself (note that the upper floor, with Elvis's bedroom and Lisa Marie's nursery, is not open to the public), customized private airplanes, an automobile collection, gold records, costumes, the check Elvis wrote as a down payment, architectural drawings, and more.

Elvis was not the big star he later became when he bought Graceland. A newspaper publisher named S.E. Toof owned the 13-acre spread and named it for his daughter, Grace. Elvis took over in 1957, paying $102,000 for it. He added an indoor waterfall, furniture upholstered with what looks like fur, a pool, and other modifications to make it as tacky as he could. (He succeeded.)

He's buried outside next to his parents.

Take note of Elvis Week ("Death Week" to the locals) in early August, culminating in the candlelight

vigil on the anniversary of Elvis's death. It is
a big deal, which can be a good thing or a bad thing,
depending on your perspective.

Check out the bizarre felt-pen scribblings on the fence, some hip-ironic, some of the psycho-lunatic-fan sort.

If you happen to be in Memphis during Birth or Death Week - January and August, respectively - sit downtown for a few hours just to watch the Elvis fans. This is the only town besides Vegas where you see people dressed like Elvis not just on Halloween, but every day.

JERRY'S SNO CONES
1657 Wells Station Rd, Memphis, 901-767-2659
www.jerryssnowcones.com
This place has every snow cone known to man or so it seems. Also served is soft-serve ice cream and delicious pesto burgers.

MEMPHIS BOTANIC GARDEN
750 Cherry Rd, Memphis, 901-636-4100

www.memphisbotanicgarden.com
NEIGHBORHOOD: Audubon-Oak Court
With over 96 acres of natural woodlands and cultivated gardens, the garden is also home to the outdoor concert series 'Live at the Garden' and the renowned Japanese Garden of Tranquility. A recent addition is "My Big Backyard." a 2.5-acre children's garden with a larger-than-life birdhouse, a tunneling adventure, a teaching pond, "leaping lawn," "critter creek," and many other spaces that cater to children of all ages.

MEMPHIS ROCK 'N SOUL MUSEUM
191 Beale St, Memphis, 901-205-2533
www.memphisrocknsoul.com
NEIGHBORHOOD: Downtown
This museum offers visitors a glimpse at the Memphis music scene from the rural music of the 1930s to the heyday in the '70s and including its global musical influence. The museum's digital audio

tour guide includes over 300 minutes of info and over 100 songs. The museum exhibits a variety of musical instruments, costumes, and treasures in seven galleries. A must-see is the exhibition about the birth of rock and soul music that was created by the Smithsonian Institution. You can learn how the white wrestler Suptnik Monroe used his black fan base as leverage to integrate the Memphis city auditorium back in the 1950s. Museum and gift shop open 10 a.m. to 7 p.m. daily. Admission fee.

MEMPHIS ZOO
2000 Prentiss Place, Memphis, 901-333-6500
www.memphiszoo.org
NEIGHBORHOOD: Midtown
Set on 76 acres, this zoo is home to over 3,500 animals with over 500 different species represented. The zoo features three zones with 19 exhibits including: Teton Trek, Northwest Passage and China, and is home to the giant Pandas Ya Ya and Le Le.

The zoo features many annual events like the Zoo Brews beer tasting from around the world. Open daily 9 a.m. to 5 p.m. (4 p.m. in the winter). Admission fee.

NATIONAL CIVIL RIGHTS MUSEUM
450 Mulberry St, Memphis, 901-521-9699
www.civilrightsmuseum.org
NEIGHBORHOOD: Downtown
This privately owned complex of museums and historic buildings celebrates the history of the Civil Rights Movement. The museum is built around the site where Martin Luther King, Jr., was assassinated on April 4, 1968. Two other buildings also connected with the King assassination are included in the complex. They have a replica of a slave ship that you can go into to feel what it was like to be squeezed shoulder to shoulder with other slaves. A mock courtroom is there for you to experience the famous Brown v. Board of Education Supreme Court decision. Another exhibit offers music and poetry from the Black Power Movement of the 1960s and 1970s. There's even a replica of the bus Rosa Parks rode the day she refused to go to the back of the bus in Montgomery. The museum collection includes 260 artifacts, over 40 films, and oral histories. Visitors can experience the museum via external listening posts that take you through five centuries of history. Open daily, closed Tuesday. Nominal admission fee.

THE ORPHEUM THEATRE MEMPHIS
203 S Main St, Memphis, 901-525-3000
www.orpheum-memphis.com
NEIGHBORHOOD: Downtown
This grand, gilded historic 1928 theater is one of the few remaining movie palaces of the 1920s, with some 2,400 seats. Now the theater hosts traveling Broadway shows during the year and features a movie series in the summer. Tours are open to the public several times during the year. (This is much more interesting than I'm making it out to be, so really try to make time for this tour.)

OVERTON PARK
1914 Poplar Ave, Memphis, 901-214-5450
www.overtonpark.org
A 342-acre public park that features a nine-hole golf course, the Memphis Brooks Museum of Art, the Memphis Zoo, the Memphis College of Art, the

Levitt Shell, Rainbow Lake, two playgrounds, and the 126-acre Old Forest State Natural Area.

PINK PALACE MUSEUM & PLANETARIUM
3050 Central Ave, Memphis, 901-636-2362
www.memphismuseums.org
NEIGHBORHOOD: Chickasaw Gardens
Built as a private residence by Clarence Saunders, the man who introduced Piggly Wiggly, the mansion has now been transformed into a major science and historical museum. Here you'll find exhibits ranging from archeology to chemistry displaying everything from shrunken heads to animatronic dinosaurs. The Planetarium features a 165-seat theater-in-the-round auditorium and projects star fields, images, and laser

images on the domed ceiling. The venue also includes an IMAX Theater, which opened in 1995 with a four-story movable screen. Open daily. Admisson fee determined by number of venues visited.

REDBIRDS
198 Union Ave, Memphis, 901-721-6050
www.memphisredbirds.com
NEIGHBORHOOD: Downtown
The Cardinals Triple-A affiliate plays at a snazzy downtown stadium, complete with the sort of contests and fans-on-field participation you get when you cross corporate America and minor league baseball. (The Burger King-sponsors a race where contestants dress as hamburger buns and make a human burger.) The home games are played at AutoZone Park in

downtown Memphis. The club offers several community programs and operates the Memphis Redbirds Foundations that funds a program that enables local children to participate in sports.

MEEMAN-SHELBY FOREST STATE PARK
910 Riddick Rd, Millington, 901-876-5215
www.tnstateparks.com/parks/about/meeman-shelby
This natural state park features 14,475 acres of hardwood bottomland that borders the Mississippi River. The park offers over 20 miles of hiking trails that are open for horses and hikers. Camping opportunities abound throughout the park and there are six two-bedroom vacation cabins available located on the shore of Poplar Tree Lake. There are 49 campsites throughout the park, all equipped with table, grill, electrical and water hookups. The park features mature Bald Cypress, Tupelo swamp, and the majestic Chickasaw Bluffs. The park features many endangered and protected plants and wild animals like deer, turkey, otter, beaver, foxes, and bobcat. There are over 200 species of songbirds, waterfowl, shorebirds, and birds of prey, including the American Bald Eagle living in the park. The Nature Center is open Fri – Sun from 10 a.m. to 5 p.m. and closed an hour at lunchtime. Here you'll find exhibits of live snakes, salamanders, turtles, fish aquariums, and an indoor live butterfly garden. The park is also home to a 36-hole disc golf course that is divided into two 18-hole courses.

STAX MUSEUM OF AMERICAN SOUL MUSIC
926 E McLemore Ave, Memphis, 901-942-7685
www.staxmuseum.com
NEIGHBORHOOD: Southside
Housed in the former **Capitol Theatre**, this is a replica of the Stax recording studio and a museum dedicated to soul music. The museum features more than 2,000 videos, films, photographs, original instruments, stage costumes, memorabilia and interactive exhibits. This is the same site of Stax Records where Isaac Hayes, the Staple Singers, Albert King, Otis Redding and the Bay-Kays, among many others, recorded their music from the 1950s till the company went bankrupt in the 1970s. Exhibits include: the Soul Train dance floor and Hayes's restored 1972 gold-trimmed peacock-blue Cadillac El Dorado. The building also houses The Soulsville Charter School. Nominal admission fee. Open Tues – Sun, closed Mon. The gift shop is worth a little extra time.

TOPS GALLERY
400 South Front, Memphis, 901-340-0134
www.topsgallery.com
NEIGHBORHOOD: Downtown
This old industrial building has been converted into a showcase for contemporary art. Down in the basement in what used to be a room used for storing coal you'll find exhibits featuring work of artists such as Chris Dorland, Corinne Jones, Sarah Jones, Seth Kelly, Lester Merriweather, Terri Phillips, Walter Robinson, Victoria Sambunaris, Igor Siddiqui, and Dan Torop. Open Saturdays: 1 – 6 p.m. or by appointment.

Chapter 6
SHOPPING & SERVICES

BURKE'S BOOK STORE
936 Cooper St, Memphis, 901-278-7484
www.burkesbooks.com/
Cozy, neighborhood bookstore that features a large selection of Memphis authors and books about Memphis. They also have shelves of cheap

paperbacks and a table of free books (free after you spend $10).

CROSSTOWN ARTS
422 N Cleveland, Memphis, 901-507-8030
www.crosstownarts.org
NEIGHBORHOOD: Crosstown; Med District
This is a performance and exhibition venue that promotes a variety of mediums including exhibition, performance, production, education, and retail. The space is open for artists and performers to host arts-related events. You might find a bluegrass band playing one week and an all-drag dance show the next.

GINO PAMBIANCHI
www.ginopambianchi.com
Pambianchi is a Memphis-based illustrator, screen printer and designer. Visit his website or contact him to drop in at his workspace where you can find him drawing.

GONER RECORDS
2152 Young Ave, Memphis, 901-722-0095
www.goner-records.com
This record shop is legendary and features a large variety of bands and artist under the Goner Records label.

JARED SMALL
DAVID LUSK GALLERY
4540 Poplar Ave, Memphis, 901-767-3800
www.jaredsmall.com

Jared Small is a local painter who paints scenes of the South. His work has been described as "imagining other people's memories." Contact him to visit his home studio.

ME & MRS JONES
2075 Madison Ave #6, 901-494-8786
www.mrsjonespaintedfinishes.com
A craft boutique that offers classes in everything from painting furniture to stenciling and upholstery. Interesting selection of painted furniture.

MEMPHIS FLEA MARKET
7777 Walnut Grove Rd, Memphis, 901-757-7777
www.memphisfleamarket.com
NEIGHBORHOOD: Cordova

This large indoor flea market
Located at the Agricenter International's Expo Center, this giant indoor flea market offers a variety of wares on display from quirky to vintage, used to almost new. Small admission fee. Third Saturday of every month.

THE OTHERLANDS COFFEE BAR
641 S Cooper St, Memphis, 901-278-4994
http://otherlandscoffeebar.com/
NEIGHBORHOOD: Midtown
The funky little coffee bar is also a gift shop. It's also a great place to relax and hear some good live music. The bar offers coffee, organic teas and homemade soups. The gift shop showcases the works of local artists. Free Wi-Fi.

PALLADIO ANTIQUES & ART
2169 Central Ave, Memphis, 901-276-3808
www.palladioantiques.com

One of the best antique shops in Memphis. A great selection of unique furniture, accessories, art, and rugs. Stop by to shop and have lunch in the café.

PAPER & CLAY
486 N Hollywood St, Memphis, 901-679-4352
www.shoppaperandclay.com
This is a small ceramics studio that showcases the modern and yet very functional and reasonably priced pieces by artist Brit McDaniel. Studio visits by appointment. (Well worth a call to stop by—you'll buy something, I promise you, like her coffee mugs below—I just love the handle.)

PERIDOT
944 Cooper St, Memphis, 901-276-3999
www.peridotmemphis.com
A women's clothing and accessories boutique. Here you'll find women's pants, skirts, tops, accessories, and jewelry, a lot of it made by local artisans. A few men's accessories are offered like wallets and belts. Brands offered include: Thigh High Jeans, Hats by Makowsky Millinery, and jewelry by Carol Cox and Jay Reynolds.

SHELBY FOREST GENERAL STORE
7729 Benjestown Rd, Millington, 901-876-5770
www.shelbyforestgeneralstore.com
NEIGHBORHOOD: Millington
This store stocks everything that you might need from dry goods, live bait, cold drinks, Frisbees, and food prepared fresh from the grill. You can even get your fishing and hunting licenses here, as this is also a game-check station. Conveniently located between the front and rear entrances to Meeman-Shelby State Park.

SHELBY FOREST TAXIDERMY
5586 Benjestown Rd, Memphis, 901-493-8370
www.shelbyforesttaxidermy.com
NEIGHBORHOOD: Millington
This is your one-stop taxidermy shop as they do everything including birds, fish, and mammals. Their motto is "the taxidermy shop that recreates your hunting and fishing memories."

INDEX

A

A & R BAR-B-QUE, 15
ALCENIA'S, 16
ALCHEMY BAR, 18
American, 20, 22, 31
ANDREW MICHAEL ITALIAN, 18
Andrew Michael Italian Kitchen, 29
ARCADE RESTAURANT, 17

B

BACKBEAT TOURS, 49
BAR DKDC, 20
BAR-B-Q SHOP, 19
BEAUTY SHOP RESTAURANT, 20
BIRDS, 58
BOTANIC GARDEN, 52
BRAD'S, 21
Breakfast, 22
BROTHER JUNIPER'S, 22
BURKE'S BOOK STORE, 62

C

Capitol Theatre, 60

Caribbean, 20
CENTRAL, 23
CHARLIE VERGOS' RENDEZVOUS, 24
CLUB 152 ON BEALE, 42
CLUB RUMBA, 43
CORKY'S, 22
COZY CORNER, 25
CROSSTOWN ARTS, 63

D

Dancing Pigs BBQ, 19
DAVID LUSK GALLERY, 63
Deli, 38

E

Eighty3, 9

F

FLEA MARKET, 64
FOUR WAY, 26
FULL GOSPEL TABERNACLE CHURCH, 50

G

GIBSON DONUTS, 27
GINO PAMBIANCHI, 63
GONER RECORDS, 63
GRACELAND, 50
GUS'S WORLD FAMOUS FRIED CHICKEN, 27

H

HOG & HOMINY, 28
HOTWIRE, 7

I

IRIS, 29
Italian, 18

J

JAMES LEE HOUSE, 8
JARED SMALL, 63
JERRY'S SNO CONES, 52

K

KINGS PALACE CAFE'S ABSINTHE ROOM, 43

L

LAFAYETTE'S MUSIC ROOM, 31
LAS TORTUGAS DELI MEXICANA, 30
LITTLE PIGS, 36

M

MADISON HOTEL, 9
ME & MRS JONES, 64
MEEMAN-SHELBY FOREST STATE PARK, 59
Mexican, 30
MOLLIE FONTAINE LOUNGE, 44

N

NATIONAL CIVIL RIGHTS, 55

O

ORPHEUM THEATRE, 56
OTHERLANDS COFFEE BAR, 65
OVERTON PARK, 56

P

PALLADIO ANTIQUES & ART, 65
PAPER & CLAY, 66
PAULA AND RAIFORD'S DISCO, 45
Payne's Original Bar-B-Que, 5, 32
PEABODY HOTEL, 10
PERIDOT, 67
PINK PALACE, 57
PRICELINE, 7

R

ROCK N SOUL MUSEUM, 53
ROULHAC MANSION, 11
RUM BOOGIE CAFÉ, 44

S

Seafood, 38
SECOND LINE, 33
SHELBY FOREST GENERAL STORE, 68
SHELBY FOREST TAXIDERMY, 69
SILLY GOOSE, 45
SLEEP INN AT COURT SQUARE, 11
SOUL FISH CAFÉ, 34
STAX MUSEUM, 60
SWEET GRASS, 35

T

TALBOT HEIRS, 12
Tapas, 18, 38
TOM'S, 36
TOPS, 37
TOPS GALLERY, 61
TSUNAMI, 38
Twilight Sky Terrace, 9

W

WILD BILL'S, 46

Y

YOUNG AVENUE DELI, 38

Z

ZOO, 54

Other Books by the Same Author

Compiler and editor Andrew Delaplaine has written in widely varied fields: screenplays, novels (adult and juvenile), travel writing, journalism. His books are available in quality bookstores as well as all online retailers.

JACK HOUSTON ST. CLAIR POLITICAL THRILLERS

On Election night, as China and Russia mass soldiers on their common border in preparation for war, there's a tie in the Electoral College that forces the decision for President into the House of Representatives as mandated by the Constitution.

The incumbent Republican President, working through his Aide for Congressional Liaison, uses the Keystone File, which contains dirt on every member of Congress, to blackmail members into supporting the Republican candidate.

The action runs from Election Night in November to Inauguration Day on January 20.

Jack Houston St. Clair runs a small detective agency in Miami. His father is Florida Governor Sam Houston St. Clair, the Republican candidate. While he tries to help his dad win the election, Jack also gets hired to follow up on some suspicious wire transfers involving drug smugglers, leading him to a sunken narco-sub off Key West that has $65 million in cash in its hull.

THE ADVENTURES OF SHERLOCK HOLMES IV

In this series, the original Sherlock Holmes's great-great-great grandson solves crimes and mysteries in the present day, working out of the boutique hotel he owns on South Beach.

THE BORNHOLM DIAMOND
A mysterious Swedish nobleman requests a meeting to discuss a matter of such serious importance that it may threaten the line of succession in one of the oldest royal houses in Europe.

THE RED-HAIRED MAN
A man with a shock of red hair calls on Sherlock Holmes to solve the mystery of the Red-haired League.

THE CLEVER ONE
A former nun who, while still very devout, has renounced her vows so that she could "find a life, and possibly love, in the real world." She comes to Holmes in hopes that he can find out what happened to the man who promised to marry her, but mysteriously disappeared moments before their wedding.

THE COPPER BEECHES
A nanny reaches out to Sherlock Holmes seeking his advice on whether she should take a new position when her prospective employer has demanded that she cut her hair as part of the job.

THE MAN WITH THE TWISTED LIP
In what seems to be the case of a missing person, Sherlock Holmes navigates his way through a maze of perplexing clues that leads him through a sinister world to a surprising conclusion

THE DEVIL'S FOOT
Holmes's doctor orders him to take a short holiday in Key West, and while there, Holmes is called on to look into a case in which three people involved in a Santería ritual died with no explanation.

THE BOSCOMBE VALLEY MYSTERY
Sherlock Holmes and Watson are called to a remote area of Florida overlooking Lake Okeechobee to investigate a murder where all the evidence points to the victim's son as the killer. Holmes, however, is not so sure.

THE SIX NAPOLEONS
Inspector Lestrade calls on Holmes to help him figure out why a madman would go around Miami breaking into homes and businesses to destroy cheap busts of the French Emperor. It all seems very insignificant to Holmes—until, of course, a murder occurs.

DELAPLAINE TRAVEL GUIDES

THE LONG WEEKEND SERIES

Delaplaine Travel Guides represent the author's take on some of the many cities he's visited and many of which he has called home (for months or even years) during a lifetime of travel.

Print and Ebook editions are updated 3 times a year.

These editions (and others as well) are available in ebook editions (from $2.99 to $3.99) or print editions (from $7.95 to $8.95, depending on city) at online retailers everywhere:

The Delaplaine Long Weekend Guide

Annapolis
Appalachicola
Atlanta
Austin
Berlin
Beverly Hills
Birmingham
Boston
Brooklyn
Cancún (Mexico)
Cannes
Cape Cod
Charleston
Charlotte
Chicago
Clearwater – St. Petersburg
Coral Gables
El Paso
Fort Lauderdale
Fort Myers & Sanibel
Gettysburg

Hamptons, The
Hilton Head
Hollywood – West Hollywood
Hood River (Ore.)
Jacksonville
Key West & the Florida Keys
Lima (Peru)
London
Los Angeles / Downtown
Las Vegas
Louisville
Marseille
Martha's Vineyard
Memphis
Mérida (Mexico)
Mexico City
Miami & South Beach
Milwaukee
Myrtle Beach
Nantucket
Napa Valley
Naples & Marco Island
Nashville
New Orleans
New York / Brooklyn
Nee York / The Bronx
New York / Downtown
New York / Midtown
New York / Queens
New York / Upper East Side
New York / Upper West Side
Orlando & the Theme Parks
Palm Beach
Panama City (Fla.)
Paris
Pensacola
Philadelphia
Portland (Ore.)
Provincetown
Rio de Janeiro
San Francisco
San Juan
Santa Monica & Venice
Sarasota
Savannah
Seattle
Sonoma County

Tampa Bay
Venice (Calif.)
Washington, D.C.
West Hollywood & Hollywood

Made in the USA
Middletown, DE
13 December 2017